Henry Wadsworth Longfellow

Kéramos

And Other Poems

Henry Wadsworth Longfellow

Kéramos
And Other Poems

ISBN/EAN: 9783744705455

Printed in Europe, USA, Canada, Australia, Japan

Cover: Foto ©Thomas Meinert / pixelio.de

More available books at **www.hansebooks.com**

KÉRAMOS

AND OTHER POEMS

HENRY WADSWORTH LONGFELLOW

GEORGE ROUTLEDGE AND SONS

1878

CONTENTS.

TRANSLATIONS.

SEVEN SONNETS AND A CANZONE, FROM THE ITALIAN OF MICHAEL ANGELO.

KÉRAMOS.

KÉRAMOS

✝ KÉRAMOS.

Turn, turn, my wheel ! Turn round and round
Without a pause, without a sound :
   So spins the flying world away !
This clay, well mixed with marl and sand,
Follows the motion of my hand ;
For some must follow, and some command,
   Though all are made of clay !

Thus sang the Potter at his task
Beneath the blossoming hawthorn-tree,
While o'er his features, like a mask,
The quilted sunshine and leaf-shade

Moved, as the boughs above him swayed,
And clothed him, till he seemed to be
A figure woven in tapestry,
So sumptuously was he arrayed
In that magnificent attire
Of sable tissue flaked with fire.
Like a magician he appeared,
A conjurer without book or beard;
And while he plied his magic art—
For it was magical to me—
I stood in silence and apart,
'And wondered more and more to see
That shapeless, lifeless mass of clay
Rise up to meet the master's hand,
And now contract and now expand,
And even his slightest touch obey;
While ever in a thoughtful mood
He sang his ditty, and at times
Whistled a tune between the rhymes,
As a melodious interlude.

Turn, turn, my wheel!   All things must change
To something new, to something strange;
  Nothing that is can pause or stay;
The moon will wax, the moon will wane,
The mist and cloud will turn to rain,
·*The rain to mist and cloud again,*
  To-morrow be to-day.

Thus still the Potter sang, and still,
By some unconscious act of will,
The melody and even the words
Were intermingled with my thought,
As bits of colored thread are caught
And woven into nests of birds.
And thus to regions far remote,
Beyond the ocean's vast expanse,
This wizard in the motley coat
Transported me on wings of song,
And by the northern shores of France
Bore me with restless speed along.

What land is this that seems to be
A mingling of the land and sea?
This land of sluices, dikes, and dunes?
This water-net, that tesselates
The landscape? this unending maze
Of gardens, through whose latticed gates
The imprisoned pinks and tulips gaze;
Where in long summer afternoons
The sunshine, softened by the haze,
Comes streaming down as through a screen;
Where over fields and pastures green
The painted ships float high in air,
And over all and everywhere
The sails of windmills sink and soar
Like wings of sea-gulls on the shore?

What land is this?   Yon pretty town
Is Delft, with all its wares displayed;
The pride, the market-place, the crown
And centre of the Potter's trade.

See ! every house and room is bright
With glimmers of reflected light
From plates that on the dresser shine;
Flagons to foam with Flemish beer,
Or sparkle with the Rhenish wine,
And pilgrim flasks with fleurs-de-lis,
And ships upon a rolling sea,
And tankards pewter topped, and queer
With comic mask and musketeer !
Each hospitable chimney smiles
A welcome from its painted tiles;
The parlor walls, the chamber floors,
The stairways and the corridors,
The borders of the garden walks,
Are beautiful with fadeless flowers,
That never droop in winds or showers,
And never wither on their stalks.

Turn, turn, my wheel ! All life is brief;
What now is bud will soon be leaf,

What now is leaf will soon decay ;
The wind blows east, the wind blows west ;
The blue eggs in the robin's nest
Will soon have wings and beak and breast,
And flutter and fly away.

Now southward through the air I glide,
The song my only pursuivant,
And see across the landscape wide
The blue Charente, upon whose tide
The belfries and the spires of Saintes
Ripple and rock from side to side,
As, when an earthquake rends its walls,
A crumbling city reels and falls.

Who is it in the suburbs here,
This Potter, working with such cheer,
In this mean house, this mean attire,
His manly features bronzed with fire,

Whose figulines and rustic wares
Scarce find him bread from day to day ?
This madman, as the people say,
Who breaks his tables and his chairs
To feed his furnace fires, nor cares
Who goes unfed if they are fed,
Nor who may live if they are dead ?
This alchemist with hollow cheeks
And sunken, searching eyes, who seeks,
By mingled earths and ores combined
With potency of fire, to find
Some new enamel, hard and bright,
His dream, his passion, his delight ?

O Palissy ! within thy breast
Burned the hot fever of unrest ;
Thine was the prophet's vision, thine
The exultation, the divine
Insanity of noble minds,
That never falters nor abates,

C

But labors and endures and waits,
Till all that it foresees it finds,
Or what it cannot find creates !

Turn, turn, my wheel ! This earthen jar
A touch can make, a touch can mar;
And shall it to the Potter say,
What makest thou ?   Thou hast no hand ?
As men who think to understand
A world by their Creator planned,
Who wiser is than they.

Still guided by the dreamy song,
As in a trance I float along
Above the Pyrenean chain,
Above the fields and farms of Spain,
Above the bright Majorcan isle,
That lends its softened name to art,—
A spot, a dot upon the chart,

Whose little towns, red-roofed with tile,
Are ruby-lustred with the light
Of blazing furnaces by night,
And crowned by day with wreaths of smoke.
Then eastward, wafted in my flight
On my enchanter's magic cloak,
I sail across the Tyrrhene Sea
Into the land of Italy,
And o'er the windy Apennines,
Mantled and musical with pines.

The palaces, the princely halls,
The doors of houses and the walls
Of churches and of belfry towers,
Cloister and castle, street and mart,
Are garlanded and gay with flowers
That blossom in the fields of art.
Here Gubbio's workshops gleam and glow
With brilliant, iridescent dyes,
The dazzling whiteness of the snow,

The cobalt blue of summer skies ;
And vase, and scutcheon, cup and plate,
In perfect finish emulate
Faenza, Florence, Pesaro.

Forth from Urbino's gate there came
A youth with the angelic name
Of Raphael, in form and face
Himself angelic, and divine
In arts of color and design.
From him Francesco Xanto caught
Something of his transcendent grace,
And into fictile fabrics wrought
Suggestions of the master's thought.
Nor less Maestro Giorgio shines
With madre-perl and golden lines
Of arabesques, and interweaves
His birds and fruits and flowers and leaves
About some landscape, shaded brown,
With olive tints on rock and town.

Behold this cup within whose bowl,
Upon a ground of deepest blue
With yellow-lustred stars o'erlaid,
Colors of every tint and hue
Mingle in one harmonious whole!
With large blue eyes and steadfast gaze,
Her yellow hair in net and braid,
Necklace and ear-rings all ablaze
With golden lustre o'er the glaze,
A woman's portrait; on the scroll,
Cana, the beautiful!   A name
Forgotten save for such brief fame
As this memorial can bestow,—
A gift some lover long ago
Gave with his heart to this fair dame.

A nobler title to renown
Is thine, O pleasant Tuscan town,
Seated beside the Arno's stream;
For Lucca della Robbia there

Created forms so wondrous fair,
They made thy sovereignty supreme.
These choristers with lips of stone,
Whose music is not heard, but seen,
Still chant, as from their organ-screen,
Their Maker's praise ; nor these alone,
But the more fragile forms of clay,
Hardly less beautiful than they.
These saints and angels that adorn
The walls of hospitals, and tell
The story of good deeds so well
That poverty seems less forlorn,
And life more like a holiday.

Here in this old neglected church,
That long eludes the traveller's search,
Lies the dead bishop on his tomb ;
Earth upon earth he slumbering lies,
Life-like and death-like in the gloom ;
Garlands of fruit and flowers in bloom

And foliage deck his resting-place;
A shadow in the sightless eyes,
A pallor on the patient face,
Made perfect by the furnace heat;
All earthly passions and desires
Burnt out by purgatorial fires;
Seeming to say, " Our years are fleet,
And to the weary death is sweet."

But the most wonderful of all
The ornaments on tomb or wall
That grace the fair Ausonian shores
Are those the faithful earth restores,
Near some Apulian town concealed,
In vineyard or in harvest field,—
Vases and urns and bas-reliefs,
Memorials of forgotten griefs,
Or records of heroic deeds
Of demigods and mighty chiefs :
Figures that almost move and speak,

And, buried amid mould and weeds,
Still in their attitudes attest
The presence of the graceful Greek,—
Achilles in his armor dressed,
Alcides with the Cretan bull,
Aphrodite with her boy,
Or lovely Helena of Troy,
Still living and still beautiful.

Turn, turn, my wheel !   'Tis nature's plan
The child should grow into the man,
　　The man grow wrinkled, old, and gray ;
In youth the heart exalts and sings,
The pulses leap, the feet have wings ;
In age the cricket chirps, and brings
　　The harvest home of day.

And now the winds that southward blow,
And cool the hot Sicilian isle,

Bear me away. I see below
The long line of the Libyan Nile,
Flooding and feeding the parched lands
With annual ebb and overflow,   ·
A fallen palm whose branches lie
Beneath the Abyssinian sky,
Whose roots are in Egyptian sands.
On either bank huge water-wheels,
Belted with jars and dripping weeds,
Send forth their melancholy moans,
As if, in their gray mantles hid,
Dead anchorites of the Thebaid
Knelt on the shore and told their beads,
Beating their breasts with loud appeals
And penitential tears and groans.

This city, walled and thickly set
With glittering mosque and minaret,
Is Cairo, in whose gay bazaars
The dreaming traveller first inhales

The perfume of Arabian gales,
And sees the fabulous earthen jars,
Huge as were those wherein the maid
Morgiana found the Forty Thieves
Concealed in midnight ambuscade ;
And seeing, more than half believes
The fascinating tales that run
Through all the Thousand Nights and One,
Told by the fair Scheherezade.

More strange and wonderful than these
Are the Egyptian deities,
Ammon, and Emoth, and the grand
Osiris, holding in his hand
The lotus; Isis, crowned and veiled ;
The sacred Ibis, and the Sphinx ;
Bracelets with blue enamelled links ;
The Scarabee in emerald mailed,
Or spreading wide his funeral wings ;
Lamps that perchance their night-watch kept

O'er Cleopatra while she slept,—
All plundered from the tombs of kings.

Turn, turn, my wheel! The human race,
Of every tongue, of every place,
　　Caucasian, Coptic, or Malay,
All that inhabit this great earth,
Whatever be their rank or worth,
Are kindred and allied by birth,
　　And made of the same clay.

O'er desert sands, o'er gulf and bay,
O'er Ganges and o'er Himalay,
Bird-like I fly, and flying sing,
To flowery kingdoms of Cathay,
And bird-like poise on balanced wing
Above the town of King-te-tching,
A burning town, or seeming so,—
Three thousand furnaces that glow
Incessantly, and fill the air

With smoke uprising, gyre on gyre,
And painted by the lurid glare,
Of jets and flashes of red fire.

As leaves that in the autumn fall,
Spotted and veined with various hues,
Are swept along the avenues,
And lie in heaps by hedge and wall,
So from this grove of chimneys whirled
To all the markets of the world,
These porcelain leaves are wafted on,—
Light yellow leaves with spots and stains
Of violet and of crimson dye,
Or tender azure of a sky
Just washed by gentle April rains,
And beautiful with celadon.

Nor less the coarser household wares,—
The willow pattern, that we knew
In childhood, with its bridge of blue

Leading to unknown thoroughfares ;
The solitary man who stares
At the white river flowing through
Its arches, the fantastic trees
And wild perspective of the view ;
And intermingled among these
The tiles that in our nurseries
Filled us with wonder and delight,
Or haunted us in dreams at night.

And yonder by Nankin, behold !
The Tower of Porcelain, strange and old,
Uplifting to the astonished skies
Its ninefold painted balconies,
With balustrades of twining leaves,
And roofs of tile, beneath whose eaves
Hang porcelain bells that all the time
Ring with a soft, melodious chime ;
While the whole fabric is ablaze
With varied tints, all fused in one

Great mass of color, like a maze
Of flowers illumined by the sun.

Turn, turn, my wheel !   What is begun
At daybreak must at dark be done,
        To-morrow will be another day,
To-morrow the hot furnace flame
Will search the heart and try the frame,
And stamp with honor or with shame
        These vessels made of clay.

Cradled and rocked in Eastern seas
The islands of the Japanese
Beneath me lie; o'er lake and plain
The stork, the heron, and the crane
Through the clear realms of azure drift,
And on the hillside I can see
The villages of Imari,
Whose thronged and flaming workshops lift
Their twisted columns of smoke on high,

Cloud cloisters that in ruins lie,
With sunshine streaming through each rift,
And broken arches of blue sky.

All the bright flowers that fill the land,
Ripple of waves on rock or sand,
The snow on Fusiyama's cone.
The midnight heaven so thickly sown
With constellations of bright stars,
The leaves that rustle, the reeds that make
A whisper by each stream and lake,
The saffron dawn, the sunset red,
Are painted on these lovely jars;
Again the skylark sings, again
The stork, the heron, and the crane
Float through the azure overhead,
The counterfeit and counterpart
Of Nature reproduced in Art.

Art is the child of Nature; yes,
Her darling child, in whom we trace

The features of the mother's face,
Her aspect and her attitude,
All her majestic loveliness
Chastened and softened and subdued
Into a more attractive grace,
And with a human sense imbued.
He is the greatest artist, then,
Whether of pencil or of pen,
Who follows Nature.   Never man,
As artist or as artisan,
Pursuing his own fantasies,
Can touch the human heart, or please,
Or satisfy our nobler needs,
As he who sets his willing feet,
In Nature's footprints, light and fleet,
And follows fearless where she leads.

Thus mused I on that morn in May,
Wrapped in my visions like the Seer,
Whose eyes behold not what is near,

But only what is far away,
When, suddenly sounding peal on peal,
The church-bell from the neighboring town
Proclaimed the welcome hour of noon.
The Potter heard, and stopped his wheel,
His apron on the grass threw down,
Whistled his quiet little tune,
Not overloud nor overlong,
And ended thus his simple song:

Stop, stop, my wheel! Too soon, too soon
The noon will be the afternoon,
Too soon to-day be yesterday;
Behind us in our path we cast
The broken potsherds of the past,
And all are ground to dust at last,
And trodden into clay!

D

BIRDS OF PASSAGE.

THE HERONS OF ELMWOOD.

Warm and still is the summer night,
  As here by the river's brink I wander;
White overhead are the stars, and white
  The glimmering lamps on the hillside yonder.

Silent are all the sounds of day;
  Nothing I hear but the chirp of crickets,
And the cry of the herons winging their way
  O'er the poet's house in the Elmwood thickets.

Call to him, herons, as slowly you pass
  To your roosts in the haunts of the exiled
      thrushes,
Sing him the song of the green morass,
  And the tides that water the reeds and rushes.

Sing him the mystical Song of the Hern,
   And the secret that baffles our utmost seeking;
For only a sound of lament we discern,
   And cannot interpret the words you are speak-
      ing

Sing of the air, and the wild delight
   Of wings that uplift and winds that uphold
      you,
The joy of freedom, the rapture of flight
   Through the drift of the floating mists that
      infold you;

Of the landscape lying so far below,
   With its towns and rivers and desert places;
And the splendor of light above, and the glow
   Of the limitless, blue, ethereal spaces.

Ask him if songs of the Troubadors,
   Or of Minnesingers in old black-letter,

Sound in his ears more sweet than yours, ·

And if yours are not sweeter and wilder and
  better.

Sing to him, say to him, here at his gate,
  Where the boughs of the stately elms are
    meeting,
Some one hath lingered to meditate,
  And send him unseen this friendly greeting;

That many another hath done the same,
  Though not by a sound was the silence
    broken;
The surest pledge of a deathless name
  Is the silent homage of thoughts unspoken.

A DUTCH PICTURE.

Simon Danz has come home again,
  From cruising about with his buccaneers;
He has singed the beard of the King of Spain,
And carried away the Dean of Jaen
  And sold him in Algiers.

In his house by the Maese, with its roof of tiles,
  And weathercocks flying aloft in air,
There are silver tankards of antique styles,
Plunder of convent and castle, and piles
  Of carpets rich and rare.

In his tulip-garden there by the town,
  Overlooking the sluggish stream,

With his Moorish cap and dressing-gown,
The old sea-captain, hale and brown,
  Walks in a waking dream.

A smile in his gray mustachio lurks
  Whenever he thinks of the King of Spain,
And the listed tulips look like Turks,
And the silent gardener as he works
  Is changed to the Dean of Jaen.

The windmills on the outermost
  Verge of the landscape in the haze,
To him are towers on the Spanish coast,
With whiskered sentinels at their post,
  Though this is the river Maese.

But when the winter rains begin,
  He sits and smokes by the blazing brands,
And old seafaring men come in,
Goat-bearded, gray, and with double chin,
  And rings upon their hands.

They sit there in the shadow and shine
  Of the flickering fire of the winter night ;
Figures in colour and design
Like those by Rembrandt of the Rhine,
  Half darkness and half light.

And they talk of ventures lost or won,
  And their talk is ever and ever the same,
While they drink the red wine of Tarragon,
From the cellars of some Spanish Don,
  Or convent set on flame.

Restless at times with heavy strides
  He paces his parlor to and fro ;
He is like a ship that at anchor rides,
And swings with the rising and falling tides,
  And tugs at her anchor-tow.

Voices mysterious far and near,
  Sound of the wind and sound of the sea,

Are calling and whispering in his ear,
" Simon Danz!   Why stayest thou here ?
Come forth and follow me ! "

So he thinks he shall take to the sea again
For one more cruise with his buccaneers,
To singe the beard of the King of Spain,
And capture another Dean of Jaen
And sell him in Algiers.

CASTLES IN SPAIN.

How much of my young heart, O Spain,
   Went out to thee in days of yore!
What dreams romantic filled my brain,
And summoned back to life again
The Paladins of Charlemagne,
   The Cid Campeador!

And shapes more shadowy than these,
   In the dim twilight half revealed;
Phœnician galleys on the seas,
The Roman camps like hives of bees,
The Goth uplifting from his knees
   Pelayo on his shield.

It was these memories perchance,
 From annals of remotest eld,
That lent the colors of romance
To every trivial circumstance,
And changed the form and countenance
 Of all that I beheld.

Old towns, whose history lies hid
 In monkish chronicle or rhyme,—
Burgos, the birthplace of the Cid,
Zamora and Valladolid,
Toledo, built and walled amid
 The wars of Wamba's time;

The long, straight line of the highway,
 The distant town that seems so near,
The peasants in the fields, that stay
Their toil to cross themselves and pray,
When from the belfry at midday
 The Angelus they hear;

White crosses in the mountain pass,
   Mules gay with tassels, the loud din
Of muleteers, the tethered ass
That crops the dusty wayside grass,
And cavaliers with spurs of brass
   Alighting at the inn ;

White hamlets hidden in fields of wheat,
   White cities slumbering by the sea,
White sunshine flooding square and street,
Dark mountain-ranges, at whose feet
The river-beds are dry with heat,—
   All was a dream to me.

Yet something sombre and severe
   O'er the enchanted landscape reigned ;
A terror in the atmosphere
As if King Philip listened near,
Or Torquemada, the austere,
   His ghostly sway maintained.

The softer Andalusian skies
　Dispelled the sadness and the gloom ;
There Cadiz by the seaside lies,
And Seville's orange-orchards rise,
Making the land a paradise
　Of beauty and of bloom.

There Cordova is hidden among
　The palm, the olive, and the vine ;
Gem of the South, by poets sung,
And in whose Mosque Almanzor hung
As lamps the bells that once had rung
　At Compostella's shrine.

But over all the rest supreme,
　The star of stars, the cynosure,
The artist's and the poet's theme,
The young man's vision, the old man's dream,—
Granada by its winding stream,
　The city of the Moor !

And there the Alhambra still recalls
  Aladdin's palace of delight:
Allah il Allah! through its halls
Whispers the fountain as it falls,
The Darro darts beneath its walls,
  The hills with snow are white.

Ah yes, the hills are white with snow,
  And cold with blasts that bite and freeze;
But in the happy vale below
The orange and pomegranate grow,
And wafts of air toss to and fro
  The blossoming almond-trees.

The Vega cleft by the Xenil,
  The fascination and allure
Of the sweet landscape chains the will;
The traveller lingers on the hill,
His parted lips are breathing still
  The last sigh of the Moor.

How like a ruin overgrown
　With flowers that hide the rents of time,
Stands now the Past that I have known,
Castles in Spain, not built of stone
But of white summer clouds, and blown
　Into this little mist of rhyme!

+ VITTORIA COLONNA.

VITTORIA COLONNA, on the death of her husband, the Marchese
di Pescara, retired to her castle at Ischia (Inarimé), and there
wrote the Ode upon his death, which gained her the title of
Divine.

Once more, once more, Inarimé,
  I see thy purple hills!—once more
I hear the billows of the bay
  Wash the white pebbles on thy shore.

High o'er the sea-surge and the sands,
  Like a great galleon wrecked and cast
Ashore by storms, thy castle stands,
  A mouldering landmark of the Past.

Upon its terrace-walk I see
 A phantom gliding to and fro ;
It is Colonna,—it is she
 Who lived and loved so long ago.

Pescara's beautiful young wife,
 The type of perfect womanhood,
Whose life was love, the life of life,
 That time and change and death withstood.

For death, that breaks the marriage band
 In others, only closer pressed
The wedding ring upon her hand
 And closer locked and barred her breast.

She knew the life-long martyrdom,
 The weariness, the endless pain
Of waiting for some one to come
 Who nevermore would come again.

The shadows of the chestnut-trees,
　　The odor of the orange-blooms,
The song of birds, and, more than these,
　　The silence of deserted rooms;

The respiration of the sea,
　　The soft caresses of the air,
All things in nature seemed to be
　　But ministers of her despair;

Till the o'erburdened heart, so long
　　Imprisoned in itself, found vent
And voice in one impassioned song
　　Of inconsolable lament.

Then as the sun, though hidden from sight,
　　Transmutes to gold the leaden mist,
Her life was interfused with light,
　　From realms that, though unseen, exist.

Inarimé! Inarimé!
　Thy castle on the crags above
In dust shall crumble and decay,
　But not the memory of her love.

THE REVENGE OF RAIN-IN-THE-FACE.

In that desolate land and lone,
Where the Big Horn and Yellowstone
    Roar down their mountain path,
By their fires the Sioux Chiefs
Muttered their woes and griefs
    And the menace of their wrath.

" Revenge ! " cried Rain-in-the-Face,
" Revenge upon all the race
    Of the White Chief with yellow hair ! "
And the mountains dark and high
From their crags re-echoed the cry
    Of his anger and despair.

In the meadow, spreading wide
By woodland and riverside
   The Indian village stood;
All was silent as a dream,
Save the rushing of the stream
   And the blue-jay in the wood.

In his war paint and his beads,
Like a bison among the reeds,
   In ambush the Sitting Bull
Lay with three thousand braves
Crouched in the clefts and caves,
   Savage, unmerciful!

Into the fatal snare
The White Chief with yellow hair
   And his three hundred men
Dashed headlong, sword in hand;
But of that gallant band
   Not one returned again.

The sudden darkness of death
Overwhelmed them like the breath
   And smoke of a furnace fire :
By the river's bank, and between
The rocks of the ravine,
   They lay in their bloody attire.

But the foemen fled in the night,
And Rain-in-the-Face, in his flight,
   Uplifted high in air
As a ghastly trophy, bore
The brave heart, that beat no more,
   Of the White Chief with yellow hair.

Whose was the right and the wrong?
   Sing it, O funeral song,
      With a voice that is full of tears,
And say that our broken faith
Wrought all this ruin and scathe,
   In the Year of a Hundred Years.

TO THE RIVER YVETTE.

O LOVELY river of Yvette !
O darling river ! like a bride,
Some dimpled, bashful, fair Lisette,
    Thou goest to wed the Orge's tide.

Maincourt, and lordly Dampierre,
    See and salute thee on thy way,
And, with a blessing and a prayer,
    Ring the sweet bells of St. Forget.

The valley of Chevreuse in vain
    Would hold thee in its fond embrace ;
Thou glidest from its arms again
    And hurriest on with swifter pace.

Thou wilt not stay; with restless feet
   Pursuing still thine onward flight,
Thou goest as one in haste to meet
   Her sole desire, her heart's delight.

O lovely river of Yvette!
   O darling stream! on balanced wings
The wood-birds sang the chansonnette
   That here a wandering poet sings.

THE EMPEROR'S GLOVE.

COMBIEN faudrait-il de peaux d'Espagne pour faire un gant de cette grandeur ? A play upon the words *gant*, a glove, and *Gand*, the French for Ghent.

ON St. Bavon's tower, commanding
Half of Flanders, his domain,
Charles the Emperor once was standing,
While beneath him on the landing
Stood Duke Alva and his train.

Like a print in books of fables,
Or a model made for show,
With its pointed roofs and gables,
Dormer windows, scrolls and labels,
Lay the city far below.

Through its squares and streets and alleys
    Poured the populace of Ghent ;
As a routed army rallies,
Or as rivers run through valleys,
    Hurrying to their homes they went.

" Nest of Lutheran misbelievers ! "
    Cried Duke Alva as he gazed ;
" Haunt of traitors and deceivers,
Stronghold of insurgent weavers,
    Let it to the ground be razed ! "

On the Emperor's cap the feather
    Nods, as laughing he replies :
" How many skins of Spanish leather,
Think you, would, if stitched together,
    Make a glove of such a size ? "

A BALLAD OF THE FRENCH FLEET.

OCTOBER, 1746.

MR. THOMAS PRINCE *loquitur.*

A FLEET with flags arrayed
　　Sailed from the port of Brest,
And the Admiral's ship displayed
　　The signal: "Steer southwest."
For this Admiral D'Anville
　　Had sworn by cross and crown
To ravage with fire and steel
　　Our helpless Boston Town.

There were rumors in the street,
　　In the houses there was fear
Of the coming of the fleet,
　　And the danger hovering near.

And while from mouth to mouth
   Spread the tidings of dismay,
I stood in the Old South,
   Saying humbly : " Let us pray !

" O Lord ! we would not advise ;
   But if in thy Providence
A tempest should arise
   To drive the French Fleet hence,
And scatter it far and wide,
   Or sink it in the sea,
We should be satisfied,
   And thine the glory be.''

This was the prayer I made,
   For my soul was all on flame,
And even as I prayed
   The answering tempest came ;
It came with a mighty power,
   Shaking the windows and walls,

And tolling the bell in the tower,
  As it tolls at funerals.

The lightning suddenly
  Unsheathed its flaming sword,
And I cried : " Stand still, and see
  The salvation of the Lord ! "
The heavens were black with cloud,
  The sea was white with hail,
And ever more fierce and loud
  Blew the October gale.

The fleet it overtook,
  And the broad sails in the van
Like the tents of Cushan shook,
  Or the curtains of Midian.
Down on the reeling decks
  Crashed the o'erwhelming seas ;
Ah, never were there wrecks
  So pitiful as these !

Like a potter's vessel broke
 The great ships of the line ;
They were carried away as a smoke,
 Or sank like lead in the brine.
O Lord! before thy path
 They vanished and ceased to be,
When thou didst walk in wrath
 With thine horses through the sea !

THE LEAP OF ROUSHAN BEG.

MOUNTED on Kyrat strong and fleet,
His chestnut steed with four white feet,
  Roushan Beg, called Kurroglou,
Son of the road and bandit chief,
Seeking refuge and relief,
  Up the mountain pathway flew.

Such was Kyrat's wondrous speed,
Never yet could any steed
  Reach the dust-cloud in his course,
More than maiden, more than wife,
More than gold and next to life
  Roushan the Robber loved his horse.

F

In the land that lies beyond
Erzeroum and Trebizond,
   Garden-girt his fortress stood;
Plundered khan, or caravan
Journeying north from Koordistan,
   Gave him wealth and wine and food.

Seven hundred and fourscore
Men at arms his livery wore,
   Did his bidding night and day.
Now, through regions all unknown,
He was wandering, lost, alone,
   Seeking without guide his way.

Suddenly, the pathway ends,
Sheer the precipice descends,
   Loud the torrent roars unseen;
Thirty feet from side to side
Yawns the chasm; on air must ride
   He who crosses this ravine.

Following close in his pursuit,
At the precipice's foot,
   Reyhan the Arab of Orfah
Halted with his hundred men,
Shouting upward from the glen,
   " La Illáh illa Alláh ! "

Gently Roushan Beg caressed
Kyrat's forehead, neck, and breast ;
   Kissed him upon both his eyes ;
Sang to him in his wild way,
As upon the topmost spray
   Sings a bird before it flies.

" O my Kyrat, O my steed,
Round and slender as a reed,
   Carry me this peril through !
Satin housings shall be thine,
Shoes of gold, O Kyrat mine,
   O thou soul of Kurroglou !

" Soft thy skin as silken skein,
  Soft as woman's hair thy mane,
    Tender are thine eyes and true ;
All thy hoofs like ivory shine,
Polished bright ; O, life of mine,
    Leap, and rescue Kurroglou ! "

Kyrat, then, the strong and fleet,
Drew together his four white feet,
    Paused a moment on the verge,
Measured with his eye the space,
And into the air's embrace
    Leaped as leaps the ocean surge.

As the ocean surge o'er sand.
Bears a swimmer safe to land,
    Kyrat safe his rider bore ;
Rattling down the deep abyss
Fragments of the precipice
    Rolled like pebbles on a shore.

Roushan's tasselled cap of red
Trembled not upon his head,
    Careless sat he and upright ;
Neither hand nor bridle shook,
Nor his head he turned to look,
    As he galloped out of sight.

Flash of harness in the air,
Seen a moment like the glare
    Of a sword drawn from its sheath ;
Thus the phantom horseman passed,
And the shadow that he cast
    Leaped the cataract underneath.

Reyban the Arab held his breath
While this vision of life and death
    Passed above him. " Allahu ! "
Cried he. " In all Koordistan
Lives there not so brave a man
    As this Robber Kurroglou ! "

HAROUN AL RASCHID.

ONE day, Haroun Al Raschid read
A book wherein the poet said :—

" Where are the kings, and where the rest
Of those who once the world possessed ?

" They 're gone with all their pomp and show,
They 're gone the way that thou shalt go.

" O thou who choosest for thy share
The world, and what the world calls fair,

" Take all that it can give or lend,
But know that death is at the end ! "

Haroun Al Raschid bowed his head :
Tears fell upon the page he read.

KING TRISANKU.

VISWAMITRA the Magician,
  By his spells and incantations,
Up to Indra's realms elysian
  Raised Trisanku, king of nations.

Indra and the gods offended
  Hurled him downward, and descending
In the air he hung suspended,
  With these equal powers contending.

Thus by aspirations lifted,
  By misgivings downward driven,
Human hearts are tossed and drifted
  Midway between earth and heaven.

A WRAITH IN THE MIST.

" Sir, I should build me a fortification, if I came to live here."
—Boswell's *Johnson.*

On the green little isle of Inchkenneth,
   Who is it that walks by the shore,
So gay with his Highland blue bonnet,
   So brave with his targe and claymore?

His form is the form of a giant,
   But his face wears an aspect of pain;
Can this be the Laird of Inchkenneth?
   Can this be Sir Alan McLean?

Ah, no! It is only the Rambler,
   The Idler, who lives in Bolt Court,
And who says, were he Laird of Inchkenneth,
   He would wall himself round with a fort.

THE THREE KINGS.

THREE Kings came riding from far away,
 Melchior and Gaspar and Baltasar;
Three Wise Men out of the East were they,
And they travelled by night and they slept by
  day,
 For their guide was a beautiful, wonderful star.

The star was so beautiful, large, and clear,
 That all the other stars of the sky
Became a white mist in the atmosphere,
And by this they knew that the coming was near
 Of the Prince foretold in the prophecy.

Three caskets they bore on their saddle-bows,
 Three caskets of gold with golden keys;
Their robes were of crimson silk with rows

Of bells and pomegranates and furbelows,
　　Their turbans like blossoming almond-trees.

And so the Three Kings rode into the West,
　　Through the dusk of night, over hill and dell,
And sometimes they nodded with beard on breast,
And sometimes talked, as they paused to rest,
　　With the people they met at some wayside well.

" Of the child that is born," said Baltasar,
　　" Good people, I pray you, tell us the news;
For we in the East have seen his star,
And have ridden fast, and have ridden far,
　　To find and worship the King of the Jews."

And the people answered, " You ask in vain;
　　We know of no king but Herod the Great!"
They thought the Wise Men were men insane,
As they spurred their horses across the plain,
　　Like riders in haste, and who cannot wait.

And when they came to Jerusalem,
  Herod the Great, who had heard this thing,
Sent for the Wise Men and questioned them;
And said, " Go down unto Bethlehem,
  And bring me tidings of this new king."

So they rode away; and the star stood still,
  The only one in the gray of morn;
Yes, it stopped, it stood still of its own free will,
Right over Bethlehem on the hill,
  The city of David where Christ was born.

And the Three Kings rode through the gate and
      the guard,
  Through the silent street, till their horses
      turned
And neighed as they entered the great inn-yard;
But the windows were closed, and the doors were
      barred,
  And only a light in the stable burned.

And cradled there in the scented hay,'
In the air made sweet by the breath of kine,
The little child in the manger lay,
The child, that would be king one day
Of a kingdom not human but divine.

His mother Mary of Nazareth
Sat watching beside his place of rest,
Watching the even flow of his breath,
For the joy of life and the terror of death
Were mingled together in her breast.

They laid their offerings at his feet :
The gold was their tribute to a King,
The frankincense, with its odor sweet,
Was for the Priest, the Paraclete,
The myrrh for the body's burying.

And the mother wondered and bowed her head,
And sat as still as a statue of stone ;

Her heart was troubled yet comforted,
Remembering what the Angel had said
Of an endless reign and of David's throne.

Then the Kings rode out of the city gate,
With a clatter of hoofs in proud array;
But they went not back to Herod the Great,
For they knew his malice and feared his hate,
And returned to their homes by another way.

SONG.

STAY, stay at home, my heart, and rest;
Home-keeping hearts are happiest,
For those that wander they know not where
Are full of trouble and full of care;
    To stay at home is best.

Weary and homesick and distressed,
They wander east, they wander west,
And are baffled and beaten and blown about
By the winds of the wilderness of doubt;
    To stay at home is best.

Then stay at home, my heart, and rest;
The bird is safest in its nest;
O'er all that flutter their wings and fly
A hawk is hovering in the sky;
    To stay at home is best.

THE WHITE CZAR.

THE White Czar is Peter the Great. Batyushka, *Father dear*, and Gosudar, *Sovereign*, are titles the Russian people are fond of giving to the Czar in their popular songs.

DOST thou see on the rampart's height
That wreath of mist, in the light
Of the midnight moon? O, hist!
It is not a wreath of mist;
It is the Czar, the White Czar,
    Batyushka! Gosudar!

He has heard, among the dead,
The artillery roll o'erhead;
The drums and the tramp of feet
Of his soldiery in the street;
He is awake! the White Czar,
    Batyushka! Gosudar!

He has heard in the grave the cries
Of his people : "Awake! arise !"
He has rent the gold brocade
Whereof his shroud was made;
He is risen ! the White Czar,
    Batyushka ! Gosudar !

From the Volga and the Don
He has led his armies on,
Over river and morass,
Over desert and mountain pass ;
The Czar, the Orthodox Czar,
    Batyushka ! Gosudar !

He looks from the mountain-chain
Toward the seas, that cleave in twain
The continents ; his hand
Points southward o'er the land
Of Roumili ! O Czar,
    Batyushka ! Gosudar !

And the words break from his lips:
" I am the builder of ships,
And my ships shall sail these seas
To the Pillars of Hercules!
I say it; the White Czar,
　　Batyushka! Gosudar!

" The Bosphorus shall be free;
It shall make room for me;
And the gates of its water-streets
Be unbarred before my fleets.
I say it; the White Czar,
　　Batyushka! Gosudar!

" And the Christian shall no more
Be crushed, as heretofore,
Beneath thine iron rule,
O Sultan of Istamboul!
I swear it! I the Czar,
　　Batyushka! Gosudar! "

　　　　　　　　　　　　G

DELIA.

Sweet as the tender fragrance that survives,
When martyred flowers breathe out their little
lives,
Sweet as a song that once consoled our pain,
But never will be sung to us again,
Is thy remembrance.   Now the hour of rest
Hath come to thee.   Sleep, darling; it is best.

A BOOK OF SONNETS.

PART SECOND.

.

☩ NATURE.

As a fond mother, when the day is o'er,
   Leads by the hand her little child to bed,
   Half willing, half reluctant to be led,
   And leave his broken playthings on the floor,
Still gazing at them through the open door,
   Nor wholly reassured and comforted
   By promises of others in their stead,
   Which, though more splendid, may not please
      him more ;
So Nature deals with us, and takes away
   Our playthings one by one, and by the hand
   Leads us to rest so gently, that we go
Scarce knowing if we wished to go or stay,
   Being too full of sleep to understand
   How far the unknown transcends the what we
      know.

IN THE CHURCHYARD AT TARRYTOWN.

HERE lies the gentle humorist, who died
   In the bright Indian summer of his fame!
   A simple stone, with but a date and name,
   Marks his secluded resting-place beside
The river that he loved and glorified.
   Here in the autumn of his days he came,
   But the dry leaves of life were all aflame
   With tints that brightened and were multiplied.
How sweet a life was his; how sweet a death!
   Living, to wing with mirth the weary hours,
   Or with romantic tales the heart to cheer;
Dying, to leave a memory like the breath
   Of summers full of sunshine and of showers,
   A grief and gladness in the atmosphere.

ELIOT'S OAK.

Thou ancient oak! whose myriad leaves are loud
  With sounds of unintelligible speech,
  Sounds as of surges on a shingly beach,
  Or multitudinous murmurs of a crowd;
With some mysterious gift of tongues endowed,
  Thou speakest a different dialect to each;
  To me a language that no man can teach,
  Of a lost race, long vanished like a cloud.
For underneath thy shade, in days remote,
  Seated like Abraham at eventide
  Beneath the oaks of Mamre, the unknown
Apostle of the Indians, Eliot, wrote
  His Bible in a language that hath died
  And is forgotten, save by thee alone.

THE DESCENT OF THE MUSES.

Nine sisters, beautiful in form and face,
    Came from their convent on the shining heights
    Of Pierus, the mountain of delights,
    To dwell among the people at its base.
Then seemed the world to change.   All time and
        space,
    Splendor of cloudless days and starry nights,
    And men and manners, and all sounds and
        sights,
    Had a new meaning, a diviner grace.
Proud were these sisters, but were not too proud
    To teach in schools of little country towns
    Science and song, and all the arts that please ;
So that while housewives span, and farmers
        ploughed,
    Their comely daughters, clad in homespun
        gowns,
    Learned the sweet songs of the Pierides.

VENICE.

WHITE swan of cities, slumbering in thy nest
  So wonderfully built among the reeds
  Of the lagoon, that fences thee and feeds,
  As sayeth thy old historian and thy guest!
White water-lily, cradled and caressed
  By ocean streams, and from the silt and weeds
  Lifting thy golden filaments and seeds,
  Thy sun-illumined spires, thy crown and crest!
White phantom city, whose untrodden streets
  Are rivers, and whose pavements are the shift-
    ing
  Shadows of palaces and strips of sky;
I wait to see thee vanish like the fleets
  Seen in mirage, or towers of cloud uplifting
  In air their unsubstantial masonry.

THE POETS.

O YE dead Poets, who are living still
    Immortal in your verse, though life be fled,
    And ye, O living Poets, who are dead
    Though ye are living, if neglect can kill,
Tell me if in the darkest hours of ill,
    With drops of anguish falling fast and red
    From the sharp crown of thorns upon your
        head,
    Ye were not glad your errand to fulfil?
Yes; for the gift and ministry of Song
    Have something in them so divinely sweet,
    It can assuage the bitterness of wrong;
Not in the clamor of the crowded street,
    Not in the shouts and plaudits of the throng,
    But in ourselves, are triumph and defeat.

PARKER CLEAVELAND.

WRITTEN ON REVISITING BRUNSWICK IN THE SUMMER OF 1875.

AMONG the many lives that I have known,
  None I remember more serene and sweet,
  More rounded in itself and more complete,
Than his, who lies beneath this funeral stone.
These pines, that murmur in low monotone,
  These walks frequented by scholastic feet,
  Were all his world; but in this calm retreat
For him the Teacher's chair became a throne.
With fond affection memory loves to dwell
  On the old days, when his example made
  A pastime of the toil of tongue and pen;
And now, amid the groves he loved so well
  That naught could lure him from their grateful
    shade,
  He sleeps, but wakes elsewhere, for God hath
    said, Amen!

THE HARVEST MOON.

It is the Harvest Moon! On gilded vanes
    And roofs of villages, on woodland crests
    And their aerial neighborhoods of nests
    Deserted, on the curtained window-panes
Of rooms where children sleep, on country lanes
    And harvest-fields, its mystic splendor rests!
    Gone are the birds that were our summer guests,
    With the last sheaves return the laboring
        wains!
All things are symbols: the external shows
    Of Nature have their image in the mind,
    As flowers and fruits and falling of the leaves;
The song-birds leave us at the summer's close,
    Only the empty nests are left behind,
    And pipings of the quail among the sheaves.

TO THE RIVER RHONE.

THOU Royal River, born of sun and shower
    In chambers purple with the Alpine glow,
    Wrapped in the spotless ermine of the snow,
    And rocked by tempests!—at the appointed
       hour
Forth, like a steel-clad horseman from a tower,
    With clang and clink of harness dost thou go
    To meet thy vassal torrents, that below
    Rush to receive thee and obey thy power.
And now thou movest in triumphal march,
    A king among the rivers! On thy way
    A hundred towns await and welcome thee;
Bridges uplift for thee the stately arch,
    Vineyards encircle thee with garlands gay,
    And fleets attend thy progress to the sea!

THE THREE SILENCES OF MOLINOS.

TO JOHN GREENLEAF WHITTIER.

THREE Silences there are : the first of speech,
The second of desire, the third of thought;
This is the lore a Spanish monk, distraught
With dreams and visions, was the first to teach.
These Silences, commingling each with each,
Made up the perfect Silence, that he sought
And prayed for, and wherein at times he caught
Mysterious sounds from realms beyond our
reach.
O thou, whose daily life anticipates
The life to come, and in whose thought and
word
The spiritual world preponderates,
Hermit of Amesbury ! thou too hast heard
Voices and melodies from beyond the gates,
And speakest only when thy soul is stirred !

THE TWO RIVERS.

I.

SLOWLY the hour-hand of the clock moves round;
So slowly that no human eye hath power
To see it move! Slowly in shine or shower
The painted ship above it, homeward bound,'
Sails, but seems motionless, as if aground;
Yet both arrive at last; and in his tower
The slumbrous watchman wakes and strikes
the hour,
A mellow, measured, melancholy sound.
Midnight! the outpost of advancing day!
The frontier town and citadel of night!
The watershed of Time, from which the streams
Of Yesterday and To-morrow take their way,
One to the land of promise and of light,
One to the land of darkness and of dreams!

II.

O River of Yesterday, with current swift
   Through chasms descending, and soon lost to
     sight,
   I do not care to follow in thy flight
   The faded leaves, that on thy bosom drift!
O River of To-morrow, I uplift
   Mine eyes, and thee I follow, as the night
   Wanes into morning, and the dawning light
   Broadens, and all the shadows fade and shift!
I follow, follow, where thy waters run
   Through unfrequented, unfamiliar fields,
   Fragrant with flowers and musical with song;
Still follow, follow; sure to meet the sun,
   And confident, that what the future yields
   Will be the right, unless myself be wrong.

III.

Yet not in vain, O River of Yesterday,
 Through chasms of darkness to the deep
  descending,
 I heard thee sobbing in the rain, and blending
 Thy voice with other voices far away.
I called to thee, and yet thou wouldst not stay,
 But turbulent, and with thyself contending,
 . And torrent-like thy force on pebbles spending,
 Thou wouldst not listen to a poet's lay.
Thoughts, like a loud and sudden rush of wings,
 Regrets and recollections of things past,
 With hints and prophecies of things to be,
And inspirations, which, could they be things,
 And stay with us, and we could hold them fast,
 Were our good angels,—these I owe to thee.

IV.

And thou, O River of To-morrow, flowing
  Between thy narrow adamantine walls,
  But beautiful, and white with waterfalls,
  And wreaths of mist, like hands the pathway
    showing;
I hear the trumpets of the morning blowing,
  I hear thy mighty voice, that calls and calls,
  And see, as Ossian saw in Morven's halls,
  Mysterious phantoms, coming, beckoning,
    going!
It is the mystery of the unknown
  That fascinates us; we are children still,
  Wayward and wistful; with one hand we cling
To the familiar things we call our own,
  And with the other, resolute of will,
  Grope in the dark for what the day will bring.

BOSTON.

St. Botolph's Town! Hither across the plains
  And fens of Lincolnshire, in garb austere,
  There came a Saxon monk, and founded here
  A Priory, pillaged by marauding Danes,
So that thereof no vestige now remains;
  Only a name, that, spoken loud and clear,
  And echoed in another hemisphere,
  Survives the sculptured walls and painted panes.
St. Botolph's Town! Far over leagues of land
  And leagues of sea looks forth its noble tower,
  And far around the chiming bells are heard;
So may that sacred name forever stand
  A landmark, and a symbol of the power,
  That lies concentred in a single word.

ST. JOHN'S, CAMBRIDGE.

I STAND beneath the tree, whose branches shade
  Thy western window, Chapel of St. John !
  And hear its leaves repeat their benison
  On him, whose hand thy stones memorial laid ;
Then I remember one of whom was said
  In the world's darkest hour, " Behold thy son !"
  And see him living still, and wandering on
  And waiting for the advent long delayed.
Not only tongues of the apostles teach
  Lessons of love and light, but these expanding
  And sheltering boughs with all their leaves
    implore,
And say in language clear as human speech,
  " The peace of God, that passeth under-
    standing,
  Be and abide with you forevermore !"

MOODS.

O THAT a Song would sing itself to me
Out of the heart of Nature, or the heart
Of man, the child of Nature, not of Art.
Fresh as the morning, salt as the salt sea,
With just enough of bitterness to be
A medicine to this sluggish mood, and start
The life-blood in my veins, and so impart
Healing and help in this dull lethargy!
Alas! not always doth the breath of song
Breathe on us. It is like the wind that bloweth
At its own will, not ours, nor tarries long;
We hear the sound thereof, but no man knoweth
From whence it comes, so sudden and swift
and strong,
Nor whither in its wayward course it goeth.

WOODSTOCK PARK.

HERE in a little rustic hermitage
  Alfred the Saxon King, Alfred the Great,
  Postponed the cares of king-craft to translate
  The Consolations of the Roman sage.
Here Geoffrey Chaucer in his ripe old age
  Wrote the unrivalled Tales, which soon or late
  The venturous hand that strives to imitate
  Vanquished must fall on the unfinished page.
Two kings were they, who ruled by right divine,
  And both supreme ; one in the realm of Truth,
  One in the realm of Fiction and of Song.
What prince hereditary of their line,
  Uprising in the strength and flush of youth,
  Their glory shall inherit and prolong ?

THE FOUR PRINCESSES AT WILNA.

A PHOTOGRAPH.

Sweet faces, that from pictured casements lean
   As from a castle window, looking down
   On some gay pageant passing through a town,
   Yourselves the fairest figures in the scene;
With what a gentle grace, with what serene
   Unconsciousness ye wear the triple crown
   Of youth and beauty and the fair renown
   Of a great name, that ne'er hath tarnished been!
From your soft eyes, so innocent and sweet,
   Four spirits, sweet and innocent as they,
   Gaze on the world below, the sky above;
Hark! there is some one singing in the street;
   "Faith, Hope, and Love! these three," he
      seems to say;
  "These three; and greatest of the three is Love."

HOLIDAYS.

THE holiest of all holidays are those
   Kept by ourselves in silence and apart ;
   The secret anniversaries of the heart,
   When the full river of feeling overflows ;—
The happy days unclouded to their close ;
   The sudden joys that out of darkness start
   As flames from ashes ; swift desires that dart
   Like swallows singing down each wind that
      blows !
White as the gleam of a receding sail,
   White as a cloud that floats and fades in air,
   White as the whitest lily on a stream,
These tender memories are ;—a Fairy Tale
   Of some enchanted land we know not where,
   But lovely as a landscape in a dream.

WAPENTAKE.

TO ALFRED TENNYSON.

POET ! I come to touch thy lance with mine ;
　Not as a knight, who on the listed field
　Of tourney touched his adversary's shield
　In token of defiance, but in sign
Of homage to the mastery, which is thine,
　In English song ; nor will I keep concealed,
　And voiceless as a rivulet frost-congealed,
　My admiration for thy verse divine.
Not of the howling dervishes of song,
　Who craze the brain with their delirious dance,
　Art thou, O sweet historian of the heart !
Therefore to thee the laurel-leaves belong,
　To thee our love and our allegiance,
　For thy allegiance to the poet's art.

THE BROKEN OAR.

ONCE upon Iceland's solitary strand
  A poet wandered with his book and pen,
  Seeking some final word, some sweet Amen,
  Wherewith to close the volume in his hand.
The billows rolled and plunged upon the sand,
  The circling sea-gulls swept beyond his ken,
  And from the parting cloud-rack now and then
  Flashed the red sunset over sea and land.
Then by the billows at his feet was tossed
  A broken oar ; and carved thereon he read,
  " Oft was I weary, when I toiled at thee " ;
And like a man, who findeth what was lost,
  He wrote the words, then lifted up his head,
  And flung his useless pen into the sea.

TRANSLATIONS.

VIRGIL'S FIRST ECLOGUE.

MELIBŒUS.

TITYRUS, thou in the shade of a spreading beech-
tree reclining,
Meditatest, with slender pipe, the Muse of the
woodlands.
We our country's bounds and pleasant pastures
relinquish,
We our country fly; thou, Tityrus, stretched in
the shadow,
Teachest the woods to resound with the name of
the fair Amaryllis.

TITYRUS.

O Melibœus, a god for us this leisure created,
For he will be unto me a god forever; his altar

Oftentimes shall imbue a tender lamb from our
    sheepfolds.

He, my heifers to wander at large, and myself,
    as thou seest,

On my rustic reed to play what I will, hath per-
    mitted.

MELIBŒUS.

Truly I envy not, I marvel rather ; on all sides

In all the fields is such trouble. Behold, my
    goats I am driving,

Heartsick, further away ; this one scarce, Tityrus,
    lead I ;

For having here yeaned twins just now among the
    dense hazels,

Hope of the flock, ah me ! on the naked flint she
    hath left them.

Often this evil to me, if my mind had not been
    insensate,

Oak-trees stricken by heaven predicted, as now I
    remember ;

Often the sinister crow from the hollow ilex predicted.

Nevertheless, who this god may be, O Tityrus, tell me.

TITYRUS.

O Meliboeus, the city that they call Rome, I imagined,

Foolish I! to be like this of ours, where often we shepherds

Wonted are to drive down of our ewes the delicate offspring.

Thus whelps like unto dogs had I known, and kids to their mothers,

Thus to compare great things with small had I been accustomed.

But this among other cities its head as far hath exalted

As the cypresses do among the lissome viburnums.

MELIBŒUS,

And what so great occasion of seeing Rome hath
possessed thee ?

TITYRUS.

Liberty, which, though late, looked upon me in
my inertness

After the time when my beard fell whiter from
me in shaving,—

Yet she looked upon me, and came to me after a
long while,

Since Amaryllis possesses and Galatea hath left
me.

For I will even confess that while Galatea possessed me

Neither care of my flock nor hope of liberty was
there

Though from my wattled folds there went forth
many a victim,

And the unctuous cheese was pressed for the city
  ungrateful,
Never did my right hand return home heavy with
  money.

MELIBŒUS.

I have wondered why sad thou invokest the gods,
  Amaryllis,
And for whom thou didst suffer the apples to hang
  on the branches!
Tityrus hence was absent! Thee, Tityrus, even
  the pine-trees,
Thee, the very fountains, the very copses were
  calling.

TITYRUS.

What could I do? No power had I to escape
  from my bondage,
Nor had I power elsewhere to recognize gods so
  propitious.

Here I beheld that youth, to whom each year,
    Meliboeus,
During twice six days ascends the smoke of our
    altars.
Here first gave he response to me soliciting
    favor:
"Feed as before your heifers, ye boys, and yoke
    up your bullocks."

MELIBOEUS.

Fortunate old man! So then thy fields will be
    left thee,
And large enough for thee, thou naked stone and
    the marish
All thy pasture-lands with the dreggy rush may
    encompass.
No unaccustomed food thy gravid ewes shall
    endanger,
Nor of the neighboring flock the dire contagion
    infect them.

Fortunate old man ! Here among familiar rivers,
And these sacred founts, shalt thou take the
¨shadowy coolness.
On this side, a hedge along the neighbouring
cross-road,
Where Hyblæen bees ever feed on the flower of
the willow,
Often with gentle susurrus to fall asleep shall
persuade thee.
Yonder, beneath the high rock, the pruner shall
sing to the breezes,
Nor meanwhile shall thy heart's delight, the
hoarse wood-pigeons,
Nor the turtle-dove cease to mourn from aerial
elm-trees.

TITYRUS.

Therefore the agile stags shall sooner feed in the
ether,
And the billows leave the fishes bare on the sea-
shore,

Sooner, the border-lands of both overpassed, shall
the exiled
Parthian drink of the Soane, or the German drink
of the Tigris,
Than the face of him shall glide away from my
bosom !

MELIBŒUS.

But we hence shall go, a part to the thirsty
Africs,
Part to Scythia come, and the rapid Cretan
Oaxes,
And to the Britons from all the universe utterly
sundered.
Ah, shall I ever, a long time hence, the bounds
of my country
And the roof of my lowly cottage covered with
greensward
Seeing, with wonder behold,—my kingdoms, a
handful of wheat-ears !

Shall an impious soldier possess these lands newly
  cultured,
And these fields of corn a barbarian ? Lo, whither
  discord
Us wrteched people hath brought! for whom our
  fields we have planted !
Graft, Meliboeus, thy pear-trees now, put in order
  thy vineyards.
Go, my goats, go hence, my flocks so happy afore-
  time.
Never again henceforth outstretched in my ver-
  durous cavern
Shall I behold you afar from the bushy precipice
  hanging.
Songs no more shall I sing ; not with me, ye
  goats, as your shepherd,
Shall ye browse on the bitter willow or blooming
  laburnum.

TITYRUS.

Nevertheless, this night together with me canst
   thou rest thee
Here on the verdant leaves; for us there are
   mellowing apples,
Chestnuts soft to the touch, and clouted cream in
   abundance;
And the high roofs now of the villages smoke in
   the distance,
And from the lofty mountains are falling larger
   the shadows.

OVID IN EXILE,

AT TOMIS, IN BESSARABIA, NEAR THE MOUTHS OF THE DANUBE.

TRISTIA, Book III., Elegy X.

SHOULD any one there in Rome remember Ovid
    the exile,
And, without me, my name still in the city
    survive;

Tell him that under stars which never set in the
    ocean
I am existing still, here in a barbarous land.

Fierce Sarmatians encompass me round, and the
    Bessi and Getæ;
Names how unworthy to be sung by a genius
    like mine!

Yet when the air is warm, intervening Ister
    defends us:
He, as he flows, repels inroads of war with his
    waves.

But when the dismal winter reveals its hideous
    aspect,
When all the earth becomes white with a
    marble-like frost;

And when Boreas is loosed, and the snow hurled
    under Arcturus,
Then these nations, in sooth, shudder and
    shiver with cold.

Deep lies the snow, and neither the sun nor the
    rain can dissolve it;
Boreas hardens it still, makes it forever re-
    main.

Hence, ere the first has melted away, another
    succeeds it,
And two years it is wont, in many places, to
    lie.

And so great is the power of the North-wind
    awakened, it levels
Lofty towers with the ground, roofs uplifted
    bears off.

Wrapped in skins, and with trousers sewed, they
    contend with the weather,
And their faces alone of the whole body are
    seen.

Often their tresses, when shaken, with pendent
    icicles tinkle,
And their whitened beards shine with the
    gathering frost.

Wines consolidate stand, preserving the form of
    the vessels ;
No more draughts of wine,—pieces presented
    they drink.

Why should I tell you how all the rivers are
    frozen and solid,
And from out of the lake frangible water is
    dug ?

Ister,—no narrower stream than the river that
    bears the papyrus,—
Which through its many mouths mingles its
    waves with the deep ;

Ister, with hardening winds, congeals its cerulean
    waters,
Under a roof of ice, winding its way to the
    sea.

There where ships have sailed, men go on foot;
and the billows,
Solid made by the frost, hoof-beats of horses
indent.

Over unwonted bridges, with water gliding beneath them,
The Sarmatian steers drag their barbarian
carts.

Scarcely shall I be believed; yet when naught
is gained by a falsehood,
Absolute credence then should to a witness be
given.

I have beheld the vast Black Sea of ice all com-
pacted,
And a slippery crust pressing its motionless
tides.

'T is not enough to have seen, I have trodden
   this indurate ocean;
 Dry shod passed my foot over its uppermost
   wave.

If thou hadst had of old such a sea as this is
   Leander!
 Then thy death had not been charged as a
   crime to the Strait.

Nor can the curvéd dolphins uplift themselves
   from the water;
 All their struggles to rise merciless winter
   prevents;

And though Boreas sound with roar of wings in
   commotion,
 In the blockaded gulf never a wave will there
   be;

And the ships will stand hemmed in by the frost,
    as in marble,
Nor will the oar have power through the stiff
    waters to cleave.

Fast-bound in the ice have I seen the fishes
    adhering,
Yet notwithstanding this some of them still
    were alive.

Hence, if the savage strength of omnipotent
    Boreas freezes
Whether the salt-sea wave, whether the refluent
    stream,—

Straightway,—the Ister made level by arid blasts
    of the North-wind,—
Comes the barbaric foe borne on his swift-
    footed steed;

Foe, that powerful made by his steed and his
    far-flying arrows,
All the neighboring land void of inhabitants
    makes.

Some take flight, and none being left to defend
    their possessions,
Unprotected, their goods pillage and plunder
    become;

Cattle and creaking carts, the little wealth of the
    country,
And what riches beside indigent peasants
    possess.

Some as captives are driven along, their hands
    bound behind them,
Looking backward in vain toward their Lares
    and lands.

Others, transfixed with barbèd arrows, in agony
    perish,
For the swift arrow-heads all have in poison
    been dipped.

What they cannot carry or lead away they
    demolish,
And the hostile flames burn up the innocent
    cots.

Even when there is peace, the fear of war is
    impending;
None, with the ploughshare pressed, furrows
    the soil any more.

Either this region sees, or fears a foe that it sees
    not,
And the sluggish land slumbers in utter
    neglect.

No sweet grape lies hidden here in the shade of
its vine-leaves,
No fermenting must fills and overflows the
deep vats.

Apples the region denies; nor would Acontius
have found here
Aught upon which to write words for his
mistress to read.

Naked and barren plains without leaves or trees
we behold here,—
Places, alas! unto which no happy man would
repair.

Since then this mighty orb lies open so wide
upon all sides,
Has this region been found only my prison
to be?

TRISTIA, Book III., Elegy XII.

Now the zephyrs diminish the cold, and the
    year being ended,
Winter Mæotian seems longer than ever before;

And the Ram that bore unsafely the burden of
    Helle,
Now makes the hours of the day equal with
    those of the night.

Now the boys and the laughing girls the violet
    gather,
Which the fields bring forth, nobody sowing
    the seed.

Now the meadows are blooming with flowers of
    various colors,
And with untaught throats carol the garrulous
    birds.

K

Now the swallow, to shun the crime of her
merciless mother,
Under the rafters builds cradles and dear little
homes;

And the blade that lay hid, covered up in the
furrows of Ceres,
Now from the tepid ground raises its delicate
head.

Where there is ever a vine, the bud shoots forth
from the tendrils,
But from the Getic shore distant afar is the
vine!

Where there is ever a tree, on the tree the
branches are swelling,
But from the Getic land distant afar is the
tree!

Now it is holiday there in Rome, and to games in
    due order
Give place the windy wars of the vociferous
    bar.

Now they are riding the horses; with light arms
    now they are playing,
Now with the ball, and now round rolls the
    swift-flying hoop :

Now, when the young athlete with flowing oil is
    anointed,
He in the Virgin's Fount bathes, overwearied,
    his limbs.

Thrives the stage; and applause, with voices at
    variance, thunders,
And the Theatres three for the three Forums
    resound.

Four times happy is he, and times without num-
 ber is happy,
Who the city of Rome, uninterdicted, en-
 joys.

But all I see is the snow in the vernal sunshine
 dissolving,
And the waters no more delved from the indurate lake.

Nor is the sea now frozen, nor as before o'er the
 Ister
Comes the Sarmatian boor driving his stridu-
 lous cart.

Hitherward, nevertheless, some keels already are
 steering,
And on this Pontic shore alien vessels will
 be.

Eagerly shall I run to the sailor, and, having
saluted,
Who he may be, I shall ask; wherefore and
whence he hath come.

Strange indeed will it be, if he come not from
regions adjacent,
And incautious unless ploughing the neighing
sea.

Rarely a mariner over the deep from Italy passes,
Rarely he comes to these shores, wholly of har-
bors devoid.

Whether he knoweth Greek, or whether in Latin
he speaketh,
Surely on this account he the more welcome
will be.

Also perchance from the mouth of the Strait and
the waters Propontic,
Unto the steady South-wind, some one is
spreading his sails.

Whosoever he is, the news he can faithfully tell
me,
Which may become a part and an approach to
the truth.

He, I pray, may be able to tell me the triumphs
of Cæsar,
Which he has heard of, and vows paid to the
Latian Jove;

And that thy sorrowful head, Germania, thou, the
rebellious,
Under the feet, at last, of the Great Captain
hast laid.

Whoso shall tell me these things, that not to have
seen will afflict me,
Forthwith unto my house welcomed as guest
shall he be.

Woe is me! Is the house of Ovid in Scythian
lands now?
And doth punishment now give me its place for
a home?

Grant, ye gods, that Cæsar make this not my
house and my homestead,
But decree it to be only the inn of my pain.

ON THE TERRACE OF THE AIGALADES.

FROM THE FRENCH OF MÉRY.

FROM this high portal, where upsprings
The rose to touch our hands in play,
We at a glance behold three things,—
The Sea, the Town, and the Highway.

And the Sea says : My shipwrecks fear ;
I drown my best friends in the deep ;
And those who braved my tempests, here
Among my sea-weeds lie asleep !

The Town says : I am filled and fraught
With tumult and with smoke and care ;
My days with toil are overwrought,
And in my nights I gasp for air.

The Highway says : My wheel-tracks guide
To the pale climates of the North ;
Where my last milestone stands abide
The people to their death gone forth.

Here, in the shade, this life of ours,
Full of delicious air, glides by
Amid a multitude of flowers
As countless as the stars on high ;

These red-tiled roofs, this fruitful soil,
Bathed with an azure all divine,
Where springs the tree that gives us oil,
The grape that giveth us the wine ;

Beneath these mountains stripped of trees,
Whose tops with flowers are covered o'er,
Where springtime of the Hesperides
Begins, but endeth nevermore ;

Under these leafy vaults and walls,
That unto gentle sleep persuade;
This rainbow of the waterfalls,
Of mingled mist and sunshine made;

Upon these shores, where all invites,
We live our languid life apart;
This air is that of life's delights,
The festival of sense and heart;

This limpid space of time prolong,
Forget to-morrow in to-day,
And leave unto the passing throng
The Sea, the Town, and the Highway.

TO MY BROOKLET.

FROM THE FRENCH OF DUCIS.

Thou brooklet, all unknown to song,
Hid in the covert of the wood!
Ah, yes, like thee I fear the throng,
Like thee I love the solitude.

O brooklet, let my sorrows past
Lie all forgotten in their graves,
Till in my thoughts remain at last
Only thy peace, thy flowers, thy waves.

The lily by thy margin waits;—
The nightingale, the marguerite;
In shadow here he meditates
His nest, his love, his music sweet.

Near thee the self-collected soul
Knows naught of error or of crime ;
Thy waters, murmuring as they roll,
Transform his musings into rhyme.

Ah, when, on bright autumnal eves,
Pursuing still thy course, shall I
List the soft shudder of the leaves,
And hear the lapwing's plaintive cry ?

BARRÉGES.

FROM THE FRENCH OF LEFRANC DE POMPIGNAN.

I LEAVE you, ye cold mountain chains,
Dwelling of warriors stark and frore !
You, may these eyes behold no more,
Save on the horizon of our plains.

Vanish, ye frightful, gloomy views !
Ye rocks that mount up to the clouds !
Of skies, enwrapped in misty shrouds,
Impracticable avenues !

Ye torrents, that with might and main
Break pathways through the rocky walls,
With your terrific waterfalls
Fatigue no more my weary brain !

Arise, ye landscapes full of charms,
Arise, ye pictures of delight!
Ye brooks, that water in your flight
The flowers and harvests of our farms!

You I perceive, ye meadows green,
Where the Garonne the lowland fills,
Not far from that long chain of hills,
With intermingled vales between.

Yon wreath of smoke, that mounts so high,
Methinks from my own hearth must come;
With speed, to that beloved home,
Fly, ye too lazy coursers, fly!

And bear me thither, where the soul
In quiet may itself possess,
Where all things soothe the mind's distress,
Where all things teach me and console.

FORSAKEN.

FROM THE GERMAN.

SOMETHING the heart must have to cherish,
  Must love and joy and sorrow learn,
Something with passion clasp, or perish,
  And in itself to ashes burn.

So to this child my heart is clinging,
  And its frank eyes, with look intense,
Me from a world of sin are bringing
  Back to a world of innocence.

Disdain must thou endure forever;
  Strong may thy heart in danger be!
Thou shalt not fail! but ah, be never
  False as thy father was to me.

Never will I forsake thee, faithless,
And thou thy mother ne'er forsake,
Until her lips are white and breathless,
Until in death her eyes shall break.

✝ ALLAH.

FROM THE GERMAN OF MAHLMANN.

ALLAH gives light in darkness,
　Allah gives rest in pain,
Cheeks that are white with weeping
　Allah paints red again.

The flowers and the blossoms wither,
　Years vanish with flying feet;
But my heart will live on forever,
　That here in sadness beat.

Gladly to Allah's dwelling
　Yonder would I take flight;
There will the darkness vanish,
　There will my eyes have sight.

L

SEVEN SONNETS

AND A CANZONE, FROM THE ITALIAN OF MICHAEL ANGELO.

[The following translations are from the poems of Michael Angelo as revised by his nephew Michael Angelo the Younger, and were made before the publication of the original text by Guasti.]

I.

THE ARTIST.

NOTHING the greatest artist can conceive
    That every marble block doth not confine
    Within itself; and only its design
    The hand that follows intellect can achieve.
The ill I flee, the good that I believe,
    In thee, fair lady, lofty and divine,
    Thus hidden lie; and so that death be mine
    Art, of desired success, doth me bereave.
Love is not guilty, then, nor thy fair face,
    Nor fortune, cruelty, nor great disdain,
    Of my disgrace, nor chance nor destiny,
If in thy heart both death and love find place
    At the same time, and if my humble brain,
    Burning, can nothing draw but death from thee.

II.

FIRE.

NOT without fire can any workman mould
  The iron to his preconceived design,
  Nor can the artist without fire refine
  And purify from all its dross the gold;
Nor can revive the phœnix, we are told,
  Except by fire.   Hence if such death be mine
  I hope to rise again with the divine,
  Whom death augments, and time cannot make
    old.
O sweet, sweet death! O fortunate fire that burns
  Within me still to renovate my days,
  Though I am almost numbered with the dead!
If by its nature unto heaven returns
  This element, me, kindled in its blaze,
  Will it bear upward when my life is fled.

III.

YOUTH AND AGE.

O GIVE me back the days when loose and free
    To my blind passion were the curb and rein,
    O give me back the angelic face again,
    With which all virtue buried seems to be !
O give my panting footsteps back to me,
    That are in age so slow and fraught with pain,
    And fire and moisture in the heart and brain,
    If thou wouldst have me burn and weep for
        thee !
If it be true thou livest alone, Amor,
    On the sweet-bitter tears of human hearts,
    In an old man thou canst not wake desire ;
Souls that have almost reached the other shore
    Of a diviner love should feel the darts,
    And be as tinder to a holier fire.

IV.

OLD AGE.

THE course of my long life hath reached at last,
   In fragile bark o'er a tempestuous sea,
   The common harbor, where must rendered be
Account of all the actions of the past.
The impassioned phantasy, that, vague and vast,
   Made art an idol and a king to me,
   Was an illusion, and but vanity
Were the desires that lured me and harassed.
The dreams of love, that were so sweet of yore,
   What are they now, when two deaths may be
      mine,—
One sure, and one forecasting its alarms?
Painting and sculpture satisfy no more
   The soul now turning to the Love Divine,
   That oped, to embrace us, on the cross its arms.

V.

TO VITTORIA COLONNA.

LADY, how can it chance—yet this we see
   In long experience—that will longer last
   A living image carved from quarries vast
Than its own maker, who dies presently?
Cause yieldeth to effect if this so be,
   And even Nature is by Art surpassed;
   This know I, who to Art have given the past,
But see that Time is breaking faith with me.
Perhaps on both of us long life can I
   Either in color or in stone bestow,
   By now portraying each in look and mien;
So that a thousand years after we die,
   How fair thou wast, and I how full of woe,
   And wherefore I so loved thee, may be seen.

VI.

TO VITTORIA COLONNA.

WHEN the prime mover of my many sighs
   Heaven took through death from out her
     earthly place,
   Nature, that never made so fair a face,
   Remained ashamed, and tears were in all eyes.
O fate, unheeding my impassioned cries!
   O hopes fallacious!   O thou spirit of grace,
   Where art thou now?   Earth holds in its
     embrace
   Thy lovely limbs, thy holy thoughts the skies.
Vainly did cruel death attempt to stay
   The rumor of thy virtuous renown,
   That Lethe's waters could not wash away!
A thousand leaves, since he hath stricken thee down,
   Speak of thee, nor to thee could Heaven convey,
   Except through death, a refuge and a crown.

VII.

DANTE.

WHAT should be said of him cannot be said ;
  By too great splendor is his name attended ;
  To blame is easier those who him offended,
  Than reach the faintest glory round him shed.

This man descended to the doomed and dead
  For our instruction ; then to God ascended ;
  Heaven opened wide to him its portals splendid,
  Who from his country's, closed against him, fled.

Ungrateful land !   To its own prejudice
  Nurse of his fortunes ; and this showeth well,
  That the most perfect most of grief shall sec.

Among a thousand proofs let one suffice,
  That as his exile hath no parallel,
  Ne'er walked the earth a greater man than he.

VIII.

+ CANZONE.

Aн me! ah me! when thinking of the years,
The vanished years, alas, I do not find
Among them all one day that was my own!
Fallacious hopes, desires of the unknown,
Lamenting, loving, burning, and in tears,
(For human passions all have stirred my
mind),
Have held me, now I feel and know, confined
Both from the true and good still far away.
I perish day by day;
The sunshine fails, the shadows grow more
dreary,
And I am near to fall, infirm and weary.

Woodfall & Kinder, Printers, Milford Lane, Strand, London, W.C.

NEW BOOKS AND STANDARD WORKS

PUBLISHED BY

GEORGE ROUTLEDGE & SONS,

LONDON AND NEW YORK.

——◆◆——

SHAKESPEARE.

ROUTLEDGE'S ILLUSTRATED SHAKESPEARE. Edited by HOWARD STAUNTON, with 850 Illustrations by Sir John Gilbert, R.A., and a Steel Portrait. 3 vols., super-royal, cloth. 2*l.* 16*s.*

"The pen, the pencil, and the printer have striven together in honourable rivalry, combining clearness of text, elegance of illustration, and beauty of type. The result is worthy of the labour, and we can say with a safe conscience to all who wish to receive or present the bard in a becoming dress, buy 'Routledge's Picture Shakespeare.'"—*The Times.*

"One of the most important additions to the mass of Shakespearian literature which has appeared for many years."—*The Critic.*

CHARLES KNIGHT'S GUINEA SHAKSPERE. With 340 Illustrations by Sir John Gilbert, R.A. 2 vols., super-royal 8vo. ; cloth extra, 21*s.* Gilt edges, 25*s.* ; or in 1 volume, gilt edges, 21*s.*

THE WORKS OF SHAKESPEARE. Edited by HOWARD STAUNTON, with Notes, Glossary, and Life. A beautiful Library Edition, in large type. 6 vols., demy 8vo, Roxburghe binding. 1*l.* 11*s.* 6*d.*

SHAKSPEARE'S WORKS. Edited by THOMAS CAMPBELL. With Life, Portrait, and Vignette, and 16 page Ilustrations, by Sir John Gilbert, R.A. Bound in cloth, 10*s.* 6*d.* ; gilt edges, 12*s.*

SHAKSPERE. Red Line Edition, Edited by CHARLES KNIGHT. With Steel Portrait, cloth extra, 7*s.* 6*d.*

THE BLACKFRIARS SHAKSPERE. Edited by CHARLES KNIGHT. Crown 8vo, cloth. 3*s.* 6*d.*

CHARLES KNIGHT'S SHAKSPERE. Complete, with the Poems, 768 pages, with Illustrations, cloth, extra gilt. 3*s.* 6*d.*

SHAKSPEARE'S DRAMATIC WORKS. A New Edition, with Notes and Life. Printed in a new Type from the text of Johnson, Stevens, and Reed. Edited by W. HAZLITT. 5 vols., fcap. 8vo, cloth gilt. 18*s.*

SHAKESPEARE—*continued.*

THE BOOK OF SHAKESPEARE GEMS. A Series of Landscape Illustrations to the most Interesting Localities in Shakespeare's Plays. In 45 Steel Plates. 8vo, cloth, gilt edges. Price 12s. 6d.

LAMB'S TALES FROM SHAKESPEARE. With Illustrations by Sir John Gilbert, R.A. 3s. 6d.

DODD'S BEAUTIES OF SHAKESPEARE. With Illustrations by Sir John Gilbert, R.A. 3s. 6d.

THE MIND OF SHAKESPEARE AS EXHIBITED IN HIS WORKS. By the Rev. A. A. MORGAN. With Illustrations by Sir John Gilbert, R.A. 3s. 6d.

THE NOVELS OF SIR WALTER SCOTT. A New Edition, with the Author's Notes. Illustrated with the Original Steel Plates, from designs by J. M. W. Turner, R.A., George Cruikshank, Daniel Maclise, J. Linnell, and others. 25 vols., cloth. £4 7s. 6d.

THE FOUQUÉ LIBRARY. Containing the Four Seasons, Romantic Fiction, the Magic Ring, Minstrel Love, Thiodolf the Icelander, and Wild Love. 6 vols., in a box. 25s.

ART RAMBLES IN THE HIGHLANDS AND ISLANDS OF SCOTLAND. By JOHN T. REID. With 150 Sketches taken from Nature and drawn on Wood by the Author, and engraved by Dalziel Brothers. 21s.

SEYMOUR'S HUMOROUS SKETCHES. Comprising 86 Caricature Etchings, Illustrated in Prose and Verse by Alfred Crowquill. 21s.

THE BIRTHDAY BOOK OF FLOWER AND SONG. Compiled by ALICIA AMY LEITH. Containing Extracts from the Works of the best English Poets, Past and Present. Illustrated with Twelve Floral Designs by the Compiler, printed in Colours by Edmund Evans. 15s.

THE BOOK OF BRITISH BALLADS. Edited by F. C. HALL, F.S.A. With Illustrations by E. M. Ward, R.A., Sir J. Noel Paton, John Tenniel, Sir John Gilbert, R.A., T. Creswick, R.A., and others. £1. 1s.

DRAWING FROM NATURE : a Series of Progressive Instructions in Sketching. By GEORGE BARNARD. Illustrated with 18 Plates in Tints and Colours, and more than 100 Woodcuts. £1. 1s.

THE WORKS OF W. H. PRESCOTT.

—◆—

THE NEW AND REVISED EDITION, WITH ALL THE ADDITIONAL NOTES BY KIRK, AND STEEL PORTRAITS.

In 12 vols., demy 8vo, cloth, £6 6s.

List of the Volumes, which can also be had separately.

HISTORY OF THE REIGN OF PHILIP THE SECOND. 3 vols. £1 11s. 6d.

HISTORY OF THE REIGN OF FERDINAND AND ISABELLA. 2 vols. £1 1s.

HISTORY OF THE CONQUEST OF MEXICO. 2 vols. £1 1s.

HISTORY OF THE CONQUEST OF PERU. 2 vols. £1 1s.

HISTORY OF THE REIGN OF CHARLES THE FIFTH. 2 vols. £1 1s.

CRITICAL AND HISTORICAL ESSAYS. 1 vol. 10s. 6d.

PRESCOTT'S WORKS. Cabinet Edition.

In post 8vo, cloth, with Steel Portraits.

HISTORY OF THE REIGN OF FERDINAND AND Isabella. 3 vols. 10s. 6d.

HISTORY OF THE CONQUEST OF MEXICO. 3 vols. 10s. 6d.

HISTORY OF THE CONQUEST OF PERU. 3 vols. 10s. 6d.

HISTORY OF THE REIGN OF PHILIP THE SECOND. 3 vols. 10s. 6d.

HISTORY OF THE REIGN OF CHARLES THE FIFTH. 2 vols. 7s.

CRITICAL AND HISTORICAL ESSAYS. 1 vol. 3s. 6d.

PRESCOTT'S WORKS—*continued.*

PRESCOTT'S WORKS. Cheap One-Volume Edition·

FERDINAND AND ISABELLA. 5*s.*

CONQUEST OF MEXICO. 5*s.*

CONQUEST OF PERU. 5*s.*

PHILIP THE SECOND. Vols I. and II. In 1 vol. 5*s.*

PHILIP THE SECOND, Vol. III., and ESSAYS. In 1 vol. 5*s.*

CHARLES THE FIFTH. 5*s.*

Motley's "Dutch Republic."

THE RISE OF THE DUTCH REPUBLIC. By J. LOTHRUP MOTLEY. In 3 vols., crown 8vo. 18*s.*

DITTO   DITTO.   New Edition, Complete in One Volume. Crown 8vo, cloth, gilt edges. 6*s.*

THE OLD POETS.

WITH BIOGRAPHICAL MEMOIRS, ETC.

These Volumes are beautifully printed on fine paper, with Steel Portrait and Vignette, and are each complete in ONE VOLUME.

SPENSER. With Selected Notes, Life by the Rev. H. J. TODD, M.A.; Portrait, Vignette, and Glossary Index. In 1 vol. Price 10*s.* 6*d.*, cloth.

CHAUCER. With Notes and Glossary by TYRWHITT; and Portrait and Vignette. In 1 vol. Price 10*s.* 6*d.*, cloth.

DRYDEN. With Notes by the Revs. JOSEPH and JOHN WHARTON; and Portrait and Vignette. In 1 vol. Price 10*s.* 6*d.*, cloth.

POPE. Including the Translations. With Notes and Life by the Rev. H. F. CARY, A.M.; and Portrait and Vignette. In 1 vol. Price 10*s.* 6*d.*, cloth.